# Aesop's Garden

## Don Byrd

**NORTH ATLANTIC BOOKS**

Aesop's Garden

ISBN 0-913028-42-8


Publisher's Address:

North Atlantic Books
Route 2, Box 135
Plainfield, Vermont 05667


Principal Distributor:

Book People
2940 Seventh Street
Berkeley, California 94710


    Acknowledgement is made to *Aux Arcs, Truck, Mulch,* and *Credences,* where some of these poems appeared originally.


Front Cover Photograph: Don Byrd
Back Cover Photograph: Jeffrey Krolick


The text was set in 10 point Palatino by Barrett Watten at The West Coast Print Center, Inc., Berkeley, Calif.


This project is partially supported by a grant from the National Endowment for the Arts in Washington, D.C., a federal agency.

# I. FELLAH

*wie eigentlich gewesen*


(from nothing)
       it comes
going back and forth
       like parking a car in a small space
           (to nothing)
and the opening seems
     an inch of time
        rammed edgewise
           into an aeon
              is where you are
    because love is an arm
      of gravity
the car is history
         but you
       are almost
            not


now
    when more people are living
      than ever have died
you are eating
      the dust
         you kicked up
     as you passed
      history has been an idyl
it has been in that like a German university
    with seminars
         and quiet meditations
     it has talked calmly
      you have walked
        in its complex gardens
a marble bust
     of Leopold von Ranke
commemorates a history that catches up with you
    and you are caught up
         cramped
         like a muscle

                                        in a running
                                          nightmare
          the directions are cruel
      as women can be
              and sometimes are

      you stand at the bar
              listening to the piano player
                      pound out
                          "Moonlight in Vermont"
              or otherwise
                      you are absorbed
          you see yourself see
                              that you
              are the one chosen
                      to be beside yourself
                              through half of your time

          when you meet yourself
      coming back from the band
              where you have made a request
      you have been replaced
                              by the music
          the melody
                      stands
                          in your place
          and drinks your drink

      if you exist at all
          you are the bass line
              the eyeless
                          fiddle player
                              thumps out
                  as if he might quit any time

          you feel it
              coming
                  to an end
      the tropes
              have disappeared
                      from your vocabulary
              they are an embarrassment
                      you can avoid
      they were like a glass

half-filled with bourbon
         but overlain with a troublesome
             cultivation
what you have lost
         (or gained)
has brought you into a music
             where you do not exist
and you are surprised
         by the accommodations
even the broken
                 shoelaces
                         of your brooding
     retrieve a sense of fitness
and the knots you tie in them
         join your inconsequence
         to a giddy future
to the magnificence of a collapsing star

2

you learn
    that not the music alone
                    replaces you
but also the streets of the city
        and everything you do
    loving your wife
      or brushing
          your teeth
    you are you expect
              replaced by the dogs
        at large in the park
           and they are vicious

    but you cannot admit that
or treat the boils
        that erupt on your neck
    it is theory only
    and the experiments
      you have concocted
    to test where you are
         in relation
     to good and evil
      gender
        matter
      the cardinal directions
    are still inconclusive

the quadrature of space
      has condensed
    irregularly
     so east and west
      conspire
   in this hemisphere
to eliminate north
     and a tropical sun
    burns
      the permafrost

if the architecture
    of your life is studied

it will be seen
            to combine
                        eclectically
        a number of southern styles
            the exaggerated verandah
                        of the plantation house
        and the air around it
            is flushed
                with the smell
                    of wisteria

but from another aspect
    it is a Greek amphitheater
constructed of the first thirty years
            of your life
where *The Death of Psyche* is played

        you wait
                eating a hot dog
for the satyr play
                    you have seen enough tragedy
the news is full of it
                though of course
                    pathos
                            predominates
        as more people are affected
                            than you imagine
            by droughts and wars
        natural disasters dig into people's backs
                like the nails
                    of passionate lovers
but it is not pornography you came for
    or not simply so
            you want to see lust
                        displayed
            as a consequent
                of sacred doctrine
        what was called desecration
            is your desire

the play drags on endlessly
                    and you walk
        the dirty streets

                                    of the theater district
              hoping to find in dusty shops
                        and crowded tenements
                                    the action you thought to see
                        portrayed on the stage

              you could never doubt this place
                  or mistake it
                                    for it has no shape
                                    but its own
                        which gives it the appearance
                                    of an ancient outpost
                  to which generations of itinerants
                                    have returned
                        having suffered nameless
                                                      defeats
                                          in the interior

              the children who are deranged
                                          appear to you
              they have recognized you
                        as one of their kind
              they toss you the ball
                                    knowing you will enter
                                          the game
              but the ball you discover
                                          is not a ball
                        it is the object
                        that has driven you
                                          questing
                        to this place

              you tell them
                        the ball
                                    is not a ball
                  but their pragmatism
                        is complete
                                    more perfect
                        than your patience
                                    or attention

              you are in danger
                  because you cannot attend to their words

though you
            focus
                        on the original design
            and call it
                        "fame"
                                    or "redemption"
or "*the* quest"
                        the words themselves
            blow-up in your face
            leaving your retina scorched
                        and your personality
                                                destroyed

you brood of course
            you believe
                                    it was not words at all
                        that made you come
            but a pressure
                        or impedance
                        that arises amongst words

your insistence
                        on clarity
            you tell them
                                    is the flying buttress
of your unhappiness
                        and the propriety of your beliefs
            confounds
                        the inquisitioners

it is you you say
                        pointing at your interlocutors
or you
            at yourself
or you
            circling a finger in the general air

3

you are seized
                the evening
                                comes down
        on the city
                westward
masses of poisonous gas gather

        you relax for dinner
counting the subtle ways
                the city's illness
        becomes your health
                none of us you say
        (to pontificate
                it's your worst habit)
                        none of us is beyond complicity
        we make a living
                        taking commissions
on the sale of ourselves

        the city stops
                        like a bouncing ball
        at its apex
for a moment
                the horns
                        are silenced
the carillon on a church wheezes a hymn
        the delinquent city
                        is the last dense
                rhetoric
                        spoken by Quintillian
        and it is convincing
                to the degree
                                it lists
possible ways
        to construct a monument
celebrating
        the extinction
                of what was called
the dilemma of smoke
        or otherwise
                        the quoins of fire

                *       *       *

in your absent-mindedness you mumble
    *"Quo modo"*
                you are not allowed
                    a hermitage or even the isolation
                  of your opinions
so you take a job as a seller
    of encyclopedias
        it is a way
            to participate
      in the deformation of all knowledge

    you come and go
               the continent uncurls
at your feet and callouses develop
      to make this occupation
                a permanent sub-plot
    of your nervous habits

    but your economic situation is more
                  complex
      and if you let
           earth surround
as it will
      as it inevitably will
        it is untenable
          work is the opium
which allows you to pass dream-like
            from the stables of the present

and though you have read Gessell
              Marx
         and Major Douglas
    you are not curious about money
      the few things you have learned
        have left you tied
      in knots
        of rage
      and fear
    as if the economy
        were one of the minor Fates
which capriciously starves you
      or encumbers you
        with property

        *    *    *

                Marx must have been a lazy man
how else
                could he have so mis-understood
                        the psychology of work?
you are already
                        eye-deep
                in your urge
                and nerve
                your business leads you beyond yourself
                        the pace
                strained
                                to a point
                        where leisure meets excitement
                                returning
                as when the urgency has gone from sex
and you believe
                        for the time
                it is the permanent answer
                                to the question of life
                you desire
                                and you possess your desire
the ache which is only an inch from fulfillment
                draws you
                        again
                                to the brink
                of the afternoon
                        what one philosopher called
                                "the wasp of time"


        you cover yourself like hives
your friends return
                shaken by jack-hammers
                        they've taken to hand
and she comes to you at time in the contortionist
                postures
                        of a surgeon's wife
                her eyes are pools
                                all artifice
                filled from below
                                with loathing


14

you gradually begin to see
        the lives
                coming apart

    how many more will devote themselves
        to Artemus
or other purity which excludes you
            how long will you wait
                for one of your number
to begin speaking
                for you all

how many steps is it
        from your writing desk
                        to the coffee pot?

4

your fingers play
                    in a stream of history
            which runs from the city
                with sleepy imprecision

        it is not
                    a precise place
        though it might have been
                            the decision
                    was made
                                and it became
                    more a fantasy
                            than a place

        but it turns in your hand
                    to your uses
        you see it as a diorama
                    displayed at a country fair
        Thomas Cole might have painted it
                    like the dusty one
            you saw half unrolled
                    in the attic
            of the Smithsonian Institute

        given his habit of perspective
            he would have stood by the Hudson
                in Troy
                        where the college
                    named
                            for the robber baron's
                            banker
                                    stands
    north
        he would see Green Island
                not quite
                        to the mouth of the Mohawk
            where the Empire bends
                                abruptly
                        westward
    and the Frontier
                in the true sense

of that abused word
 bends with it

across the river
                and south
  he would see the riverfront
     in Albany
  his point of view
                    would be raised
to a height
   as if he were looking
                    at the valley
     from the gondola
        of a precarious balloon

beyond
        southwest
closing the horizon against the sky
        the rock face of the Helderbergs rises
           above the Pine Barrens
which Herman Melville mentions
                      in *Moby Dick*
     as a desolate
                and lonely place

   so he stands
near the center of a funnel
      which closes westward
                          along the Erie canal
        and the Thomas E. Dewey Thruway
   Cole would have used the rock
      as a reminder
        that the thriving
                       human activity
     in the valley
           is petty
against the eternally slow processes of geology

   more than once
              you've wanted to kick in
       the face of the Helderbergs
       for no more reason
            than to see the sky

                              go on
          your credentials
                         as a drug-store cowboy
                              are impeccable
               in the closet
                         with your two-toned
                              patent leather shoes
                    you keep a pair
                         of sharp-toed boots
                              embroidered
                    with a device
                                   of cacti
                              and eagles

          but the boots do not satisfy
                    your gaudy expectations
          your notion of style
                         is exemplified
                    despite all you've learned
                         by locomotives
                              from the aureate decades
                         following the Civil War
          you enjoy doodad decorations
                                   and accomplishments
          and you would still spend your vacation
                    watching a tight-rope artist
                         cross Niagara Falls
               you are thrilled
                    by your readings
                         in *Guinness' Book of Records*
          the picture of Robert Wadlow alone
               is worth the price of the book
          and though you understand
                                   his condition
                    was glandular
                              he stands
                         as the imperfect
                                   realization
                         of some Ultimate
                              Human Form

               you are the learned drummer
          riding the trains

of your imagination
through the pages
of an encyclopedia
and you consider
the reorganization of all knowledge
so it might be equal
to "Our Troubled Times"
as the Jehovah's Witness pamphlet
you find at your door
declares it
and without doubt
these are troubled times
although a *cordon sanitaire*
has been erected
around the capital
it fills with rumors
and the viruses spill over
into the rest of the city

you sometimes ask
if it weren't a mistake
when you faced into the wind
and started eastward
but what purity
is worth preserving
and what time isn't lost

if you had leverage
with the city's political machine
you would of course
pull the lever
even as the winds
of a Populist Revolution
blow in
from the open ranges
and starving cattle
in the drought
stricken
heartlands

if each fact might yield its mercy
what might be called
the limits of its corruptability

                this factual world
                                might spin
                    with the torque
                                    of love
                        in a mind
                                    that would not change
                        for thirty thousand years
and a new edition
                                of the encyclopedia
                    would be unnecessary

## 5

you come out
                under the decorous sun
        by the impromptu sea
            under the ignorant
                and skin-lashing sun
        proper beyond belief
                in the rehearsal it requires
            and the songs it sings
                    like choirs of reductionist
                        mythographers
                and tired accountants
                        whose pencils click

but you do not venerate the light
                nor do they
        who in the light's light
                spit out the seed-pits of the day
you would pull the rabbit
                        of dark passages
            from the darkness
            of the dirty hat
where the restless dreams are deep
                and long for rest
        between an illusion of morning
            and an illusion of
                        afternoon
                the unselfconscious sea
                    comes spilling through
            so the coast is bathed
                        in blue light
and the palm trees
                glow
            from within

    in this way only
            you can walk
                        the littoral space
though the sands burn your feet
            and the margins of the sea
                leave
                    your mind
                        raw

21

with their rubbings
it is not wisdom you offer
or even knowledge

only a space
                large enough
                                for love
                        to flourish
        as they say in biographical notes
                        on obscure renaissance poets
                that he "flourished about 1595
                and probably died
                                exiled in France
                three poems are attributed to him
                including the memorable
                'To _____'
        a moving declaration
                        of endless
                                        love
                in powerful
                                and forthright
                monosyllables"

        half the fools at the Faerie Queen's feet
                could turn a memorable verse
in a time of crisis
                        but your epoch
                is bereft of time
as well as the other splendours
                        1893 was the last year
and we have kept
                        calendars
                                as courtesies
                something lumberyards give
                for Christmas

        you would declare your love
                in forthright
                                and powerful mono-
                                syllables
you would say
        "I am the grey bull
        which stands
                at the end of the sky"

22

(that was the way you
                    spoke
        in those days
                    with your friends)
    when what stood
            at the verge of paradise
was as palpable
            as paradise itself

    this age
            is not without honor
                    or cause for
                                tireless
                    meditation
    but looking out now
                    across the crusted snow
    which catches the red cast of the setting sun
        you are tempted by
                    nostalgia
                violent of purpose
    the point is not to
                end something
                    ceremoniously
    already ended without ceremony
            but to clear some commonplace
                    drawers
    thoroughly democratic drawers
                            not ruthless
            in their documentation
                of biography
        as you are
                in memory
    "I was the grey bull
            because my scrotum swung
                between my thighs
    and I stood at the Gates of Paradise
                because I could feel them
                    swinging

    and tonight
            I am
                the valfather
            of my race"

6

Highway U.S. 20
           rises eastward
                      on orange
                  steel
                    girders
and slips nonchalantly
           over the banks
              of the Hudson
    where the street cages through
      twisted interchanges
the signs read like
          a page
    torn from Whitehead's and Russell's
       *Principia Mathematica*

and you wonder why
             unity
   has never seemed to you
    less than obvious
the interchanges rise
           in levels so random
  that even the careful mind
    cannot hold to the counting
  as it follows its
          programmed
             way
       past the green markers
number loses itself in mid-air
    the interchanges rise on girders
      not the mind
           caged like a murderer
      gathered
          but not composed

and you are across the great river
    before you notice
the upper stories of
         the housing projects
   command
         a view of the port
    the banana boats from

Honduras
                    docking
          calypso
                to unload


an occasional child in the Welfare Towers
            traces it
                  back
                    to the jungles
and hears the guns of a Latin Revolution

but
      if it were a plant
you'd say
                it had withered on the vine
            you find yourself in Troy
                              New York
            and you've never seen the edge of being-
                's knife so dulled
                            as here
where Uncle Sam's pickled pork gave
                                  the nation
            a symbol
                    and a Roller Derby Queen
                                          passes
                  as the italics
                        of femininity


an aggressive inattention prevails
                    a posture
that might pass for courage
                                in a condemned or
                                    dying
                                          man
but it leaves the eyes pliable
                      and the question of
                            their ownership
                                  unanswered
            so you might reasonably ask
                      Whose eyes are these?

      you can only
                believe

the tragedy
            these citizens
                        suffer
            is epistemological

            you have crossed a river
                        beyond which
            you see
    the passage
            was made at flood stage
    and you suspect
                        the sub-structure
            of the bridge
                        of being
            in a dangerous
                        state
            of decay
    it is a bridge of nerve
                        in other words
            which is crossed in one direction

    you understand
                that you have lost
        an advantage
            you did not know
                        you had
but it appears in retrospection
            and you realize
                        as you sometimes do
                before you fall
                        that you are falling
            and you can do nothing
                but trust the ground

    it is in that like a dream
                        of falling
which convinced you
                as a child
        that sleep takes place
                        at some immense
                                height
and you fall back to your bed
                        with waking

you found confirmation
        in the fact that
                you woke
                        with you bed
                                shaking
you consider
            for a moment
                        a geography
        in which there is but one direction
and that
            the way to Troy

you drive to the diner
        where the waitress from the home of
            the Cardinals
                        waits
        you growl a few bars
            of *St Louis Blues*
                            as you enter
but the melody
                    has lost hold in itself
you cannot force the syllables
                            to explode
        with your blue intent

            and she says to you
"Why do you practice
                    the asceticism
            of despair?
    which issues in
                    the singular beauty
            of solidity?
a landscape seen in despair
            is a solid landscape
a woman
        a solid woman
but beyond solidity is nothing
            but the foundation of
                    further despair"

        and the varicose veins of her profession
            run in her voice
                        you tell her

that Troy, New York
                    is no metaphor
    it is the City of Despair
and you have happened into it

she answers with
                    the moist decorative
                        eyes of one
                    who's known despair
                        in several cities
            and in forms which you believed
                only dirty jokes might take

"Dido was a fish"
                    she says
"whom Aeneas loves in his defeat
                                and flight
                            from Troy
            and as she could not leave
                        the sea
                    she died gasping
                            and purple
                    on the beach"

the steps of your breath
                            seem again
        a raucous stair
leading to an immoderate fit
            of trans-temporality
        during which
                    you follow
        a blue-tailed lizard
                across the landscape
and she brings you
                a cup of soup
                        flecked with parsley

    redemption comes
                        an inch at a time
or it is a matter of inches
            scaling a rock wall
                            offers a comparison
            because redemption is an allegory

but not solely so
        for the omnidirectional highway to Troy
            sets on earth
                    as solidly
                            as a cordillera
more rigorous than the Rocky Mountains
        redemption happens in one place
            but its implications
                            are miles away
        in another town
                    or perhaps another universe
and you spend the rest of your life
                    trying to get there

        when it appears—I imagine it
                            as a City
                    on the High Plains—
            which you see
                as lights
                        glowing
            on low clouds
                    down ninety miles
            of highway
                as straight as
                        death
it seems that you have fallen
                    under its force
and the acceleration
                when you begin to fall
        is an exhilaration
            which you have seldom known

    you understand
                as you break the corium
        from the outside
                    in
that the inner perfection of the City
        could never be inferred
from the landscape
                except in the sense
            that you escape
                    anything
            that is intimate

                *    *    *                              29

you are not far
from Athens
and the Periclean Age
speak well
speak well
you have destroyed nothing
and you have come
to a place
where
everything
counts

7

one two three
    four five six seven
        eight nine ten eleven twelve

    you could go on like this
                    forever
you find yourself writing
    a narrative poem or
                your life
                    is
                    a narrative poem
            and you are ashamed
    it is the badge of your old-fashionedness
                and proof
        you have not learned to live
            where speed is glamour
            and pace is all

    you tell them
        the encyclopedias are
                        the daily discipline
                            of death
    (they listen
        with knees drawn-up
            as tumblers
                    are taught to fall)

    the pages open to one
                        in time
        and turn
                turn
    to time in one
        and the passage between
                    is the collapse
                into a factual paradise
        where roses grow
                with no authority
            but their own

the telling of one's self
                    is told

as in a mystery novel
in which everyone
                    is the victim
                        and everyone
            even the child whose eyes
                            are as large and innocent
                        as moons
                    is the murderer
            it is the perfect crime
                        because everyone
                            is implicated

you have seen buildings constructed
                            by beginning at the top
first the roof
                is pushed up
                            gradually
            floor by floor
until it reaches heights that are not spoken of
                but whispered
                            as if it were
                    some vicious rumor

        and that is the principle
                        on which the Revealed City is built

the undeniable fitness
            of architecture
                        (in mind) comforts
                the sensorium
                            so when you enter
            where the St Louis Woman
                        waiting
            the crow's feet
                        barely perceptible
                at the corners
                    of her eyes
            give her face a depth
                    which you inhabit
                        exalting
if there were a garden
        in her face
                it would be a garden

of medicinal herbs
                as you watch her stretched
                        on the couch
                                        and her blatant voice
                recalls you to an autumn
                        in your childhood
when the Cardinals were still in the race
                        for the pennant
                during the last week
                        of the season

            the excitement
                that situation implied
returns to you now

                the City on the High Plains
                        does not exits
it is to be made of
                        your concrete body
                                the steel
            of your love
                        to reinforce
                                        the walls
                the laws
                        also
                    precipitant
                                    the mother
                of your ascetic
                                    vinegar

**8**

the syntax of places
                    shakes you
          into recognition
                    Troy is a prepositional phrase
      in the form
                    of two valleys meeting
      hanging limply
                    from an ill-conceived
                              sentence

      which leads the mind
                              further
into its complexities
                    and ends
      in a snarl of inaccurate verbs

      where
just at the edge of the
                    desperate
                    silence
      a pulse starts up
          not an idea
                    but the shape
                              of thought itself
                    emulsified
          in the dense interstices
                    of entries
                              hazardously
                    chosen
                              to illustrate
                    the completeness
          of the encyclopedia

      the unexpected freshness
the dizzy speed of synapses
                              cracking
modulates
              the homicidal calling
      with a blast
                    of intense
                              surrender

you had thought to leave Troy
            riding the rods
                            of a violent train
like those spur-lines
            into unsettled interiors
            which at their destinations
            unload
                    and return
                            in reverse
            pushing the caboose
                back to the coastal city


        ancient deep and stifling forms
rise from the unused mills of Troy
            you cannot sleep
                        for they trouble
                the shape of the space
            you bed in
                        you listen
                            to the air


        they are the goddesses of your mind and
the longing to take
                        the passionate walk
                to the altar
            where the blood of teen-agers
                        is paid
            against the increase
                of the tribe
                    and the whir
                        of the sexual mills


        you stir the fool of paradise
            into a solution of pity
the tongue
            in your mouth
                fails
                    to form
            around the holocaust
                you feel rising
                    in what may be
                        your mind


            *     *     *

until you bind him
                    utterly
          by all of his senses
                    to a rendition of a song
                          you once heard
     when you were carried into the pleistocene
               of your own haunted tradition

          you have come to live in a trope
               of the inlands
     when a family of hunters goes forth
               hungry for last things
          satisfied only by destruction
               they drive the mastodons
                    into death traps
                    and leave them
                              to predators and to rot

          until the last one
                         which they circle
                              with an anticipation
     that in its violence
               could not be borne
                    in the frames of their descendents
                    for months
               their ritual approach advances
                         and retreats
                              across the inlands
     with a rhythm
                    that paces to something
                         deep in their rounded skulls
     their eyes grow wide
                         with enthusiasm
     and a time comes they call
               "the time of the eyes"

          the acuteness of their ears allows them
                    to hear
     the intricate blood
                         which is a river
                              in hard passage
     flowing through the beast
               and that is "the time of the ears"

they say
                "We hear the small beasts
            of the soul
                    gathering on the spaceless
                    knives
            which circumcise audition"
and the song they sing
            blows its warm breath
                on your aching fingertips


        and then
                "the time of the teeth
                                comes"
as you remember
                the interior
                        landscape
of your body
            and its sadness
you find your self
                at a syntactical juncture
where your being
                is required

a bridge that swoops westward
            with the precise
                and graceful
                            violence
            of a hawk

# II. AESOP'S GARDEN

1

out
    under the blue stars
                Arcadia sleeps
        in white farm house
wheat grows to the doorsteps
        in the wild places
                Francis Parkman saw
      and fevered
                through a film of hallucination
             reported

    satyrs dancing
            on the congealed
            inland
                oceans

    westward through the edge of
        the Pine Barrens
and into the Helderbergs
                the engine of your car
        whines up a pitch
    taking purchase
            on a rope of road
      hanging tautly
        from an ill-defined horizon

    you have no destination
only the mountains
        you said
            to St Louis Woman
fleeing into a landscape
      which would not render the play
        of your loneliness melodramatic

    you are wandering
                between two landscapes
one is a womb
    because the horizons are limited
        and it is known
    as the mind is known
the other

is a revolving door
you have entered
and its arc
embodies
Zeno's paradox
of the tortoise
and the hare

after you pass through Berne
you have lost all purpose
and even motion
having entered casually
almost without thought
this place
where space is intention
you can leave
only when you mean to

all you ever wanted
was to move
from one to two
but you are compelled
beyond your measure
the compulsion is
to keep driving
and talking
to bring a region to mind
which exists in the dreams
of sleeping rocks

the distance from the Helderberg homesteads
to the Revealed City
is not sentimental
it is strategy
simply
to begin the story
after the hero dies
and is transported
bodily up
as a bridge
a mind
across the inlands

*     *     *

travel
        as a way of life
is a kind of Calvinism
                with this difference
        everyone is damned
                every mile you make possesses you
        the car seems almost
                to stagger on the grades
and you stop in a movie-set motel
        which St Louis Woman likes
                because it lacks Innocence
        and she says your practice
                of despair
                        is an innocence
                she will master
because she is the Lady of the Mississippi River

        and you hope
                that it is not some rough beast
you have led to water
                at the trough
of your liaison
                with a woman
        whose wisdom is a stream
                the mother and
                        father
                of waters
                        whose banks
        are the inner-lips
                of the halves of the continent

        you climb the tree
                of your innocence
as one might
                confronted with a she-bear
        who loves viciously
and her voice is like wind in the leaves of the trees
        you inch your way
                        into the tips
        of the branches
and never before
                has the moon seemed to you

so ripe
        so close
                so folded into itself
and beyond
        the stars dig down
            to take hold in space
         you lick the sweet moisture
          collected inside the leaves

never before
        have you known
    what thirst satisfied
            might be
zones of ecstacy
          burst from your throat
   and you see they are zones of time
       to which you are given
     you are required
          to exploit your resources

as if the congealed ocean Parkman saw
had begun to flow
     and representations are what you touch
your rough fingers
         are absolute
              and the magistracy
     of Image comes loose
        pliable
           in your hands

from the crest of each wave
      you crane upward
trying to enumerate the paintings you saw
        in the Louvre
assuming residence in the crisis

you did not anticipate
        that you might father a child
who would come to replace you
      in your innocence
or that you might share
        the breasts of St Louis Woman
    with one who has no name

and sleeps
                    unroused
                              in the rocks
whose form
               leafs
                    through the sheets oi your
                              imagination
to an unused page
                    and writes its name
          which is the name of your innocence
you find yourself                         ❧
                    sliding
                              again
                    into a crevass

between what you remember
                              and some nameless
                    allegorical painting
               which proposes a strip-teaser
                    as an emblem
                              of heavenly love

          the instant
                    before the images coincide
you find yourself
                    again at a crest
          which seems
                    more hopeless
                              than the one before
          participant
                    in an orgasm
               rising from the ground
          where time and
                    space
                              have their intercourse
          the cornerstone of the Revealed City

2

      you watch
           with an excitement
that is purely physical
    the fog
       slips
            over the brow of the hill
pushed by a misted
       rising sun
           and rolls down
ceremoniously
     into the valley
in the most spectacular display of tautological
       argument
    you've ever beheld

it seems a spell cast for you
    a ring of light against it
           a celebration


    the leafless trees cast their shadows
on the macadam road
       the sun glares
and you record the changes in direction
    and shape
     as the slow angular motion
of the sun betrays you
       in its speed and
      more precisely
        its intent


your inclination has been
         to sleep in a bottle
   or a cliff-dwelling
    you are comforted by mountains
  and trees
     which close the quarters of heaven
   to your sight
you have moved with the shade
   as required
     when you were born
you were presented with a dilemma

but you were given no opportunity
to chose
the kitsch creation
called "life on earth"
was so vital
and is
that whatever the other horn
brought to a point
was not allowed a body
or even
a voice

the inspissate aether
propounded in a perverse
syntax
was both
the in
and the out
which spins
with every barber's pole

the muddy images rose
to form the outward circumstances
of your life
you mapped your accumulated uncertainties
by the same photographic techniques
that allowed the CIA
to hunt down and murder Che Guevera
who would have been a threat to neither
their economic
nor their ideological
interests
had he not been beautiful
and let his eyes play northward
with cat-like savvy
to arouse the ardour of Miss America

you are almost asleep
the toothless poem
takes your finger
and sucks a virtue
from it
the tongue's dance

                in the mouth
                                cuts patterns
            as complex
                            as a covert operation

            to say
                    "I am speaking"
            though it reaches into itself
                                    and confirms
                        a higher fact
                                in its assertion
            is the secret agent's first law
                        he shadows his man
                        through his etymology
                                until he is located
                        in a dead language

            the furbelow of your moods
                    rankles
        at the dragons of injustice
                                and the pigs of
                                        industry
        whose swinish designs
                            willy-nilly
                                    include you

            with those for whom
                            love
        is not bought and sold
                            as coats
                                    so specific
            in their decorations
                        that they cause carbuncles of discontent
        it is the rampikes
                        and charcoal
                of a burned forest
            you gather the tesselate valances
        of an instant
                    in a sack
        as if you were picking mushrooms
                        the fungi of your epoch
        growing densely
                    in the darkening expectations


                        *       *       *

your correspondent
saw your misanthropy
                    curled around your limbs
but now it is the discord
which your harmony resolves
            curling through your music


    "Give me
            for now"
                    you say
"the rhetoric of Milton
      as when he wrote
                    'Avenge, O Lord, thy
                slaughtered saints'
and I will clear an age

      —to canvass the edge of time
to read by the light of the non-existent city
            to thread my way
        through
                    these damned elations
                        of mind"

3

you see that you have a choice
you might render
                    the apocalyptic song
            as a hymn
                        (you recall "Amazing Grace"
    as it was sung
                by Gladys Reilly
        her blistering voice
                        sliding from note to note
            in a continuous curl
        so it seemed that the Holy Spirit
                might ride it
            as a roller-coaster
                    and come fluttering to rest
            on the baptistry)

or you might
                    sequined and bejeweled
        sing it as a blue-grass ballad
            let the voice sag
    into its natural habitat
            and the local distress
    of the bars in the back streets
                of the dozen small towns
        where you were raised
            among a band
                        of unromantic gypsies
    the itinerant anarchy
                of the barely respectable

    your sentimental attachment
                to the deprivation of your up-bringing
        asserts itself
                    at awkward times
    when you claim your true heritage
            and proletarian connections
        you evoke too often
            an anglophilic
                        "Why I hope not!"
        and dark distrustful eyes
    the textus receptus

of a mode of social snobbery
which sticks in the throat
like the grease of an English pâté

—to canvass the edge of the future
seems an infinite proposition
colored by the rainbow
refracted of an instant
which is about to pass
and fading
(I am invaded
I recall the others
and the bad nights we spent
night after night
shooting snooker
especially the one
who became a gun-toting
District Attorney
and bepadlocked the movie house
and the one
in his melancholy
ate rose petals
and later went mad)

as if to canvass the past
allows an inference
traced as a straight line
from the ones who are painfully familiar
to a condition of benign accident
so a chance note
which seizes the attention
implies a world where
cause and effect
have a whacky usefulness

those who passed westward
over the Rocky Mountains
have the trusted the stability of the San Andreas Fault
as they have put their own equilibrium
to the test
you
who have ventured
across the Appalachian Ridge

have done so in innocence
                    or
                              in defiance
          of a folk knowledge
               that is totalitarian

          America is a bowl
closed east and west
                         by mountains
               and this
                    is the sky
                         outside it
          half sea
               half history you are unable
                              to forget

—to read by the light
          of the non-existent city—
     you reenter
                    the medi-terranean time
the inland sea
          of America
                         is dry
the water's retreat
                    reveals
          what was inferred
                              before
          from the way the tides ran
               what the rips and breaks showed
          the beauty
                    of the goddesses
               as they appeared

          your father's generation
recovered
               the endless
          and often
                    unhappy
               rhythms
                         of your divinity
but if everyone is a god
          it is nothing
          as if nothing

                you are left
           to inhabit
                a garboil of accidents
as the lever you are to plant
           under the edge of the continent

these elations of mind
                               continue
                     uncertainly
           but their dense remains
                                      are teeth
                biting
           into the
                     igneous core
                of the inlands

4

the awkwardness
                    belligerent
                                        awkwardness
        of love

            it is a day
                        and must
    like any other
                    offer its grandiose
            and macabre
                            solutions in time

                    you circle
        suburb to suburb
                        showing your wares
            to prospects
                        for whom knowledge
        has become hors d'oeuvres
                                to a main course
        spiced with feelings of
                        dread and
                                longing

            you find yourself
                        drinking
            in bars
    where people are serious
                            about oblivion
            the velveteen dress
                        of the torch singer
                reveals a form that might have been
                    Kansas
                                or Idaho
                    had it not been this woman
    who sings "No Moon at All"
            in a voice
                that could have been seductious
            or lovely
    but as it is neither
                        you assume
                            her talents lie

unmade
in some other bed
and you are bloodied with love

if you go among those
who do the world's business
though poorly
you are required to explain
it is less taxing
to move among people
for whom loss
and defeat
are expected
in a common way

you have come to a place called
"Aesop's Garden"
you have been waiting for this time
when all is said
that you know to say

the remainder is dark
and unexplored
like the face of W.C. Handy
he must have played piano
in whore houses
they must have noticed
that his genius was a wisp of smoke
which rose from a fire
apropos
of nothing

and when you walked
by the Mississippi River
where they built
the Gateway Arch
apropos of nothing
except the angular ascent of space
and the halves of
a continent
a valve
through which the symbolic lust

of a delinquent people
                          informed itself
                on a pathologically
                          unknown territory
      you discussed the Cahokian Empire
            and posed to St Louis Woman
                  the question
did the horses run better
                          at the track
            tuned to the chilling influences
            of a tribe that dispersed
                  undefeated


      Father Marquette
                        writes
            in round tones of fright
      when he records a Cahokian image
            bespeaking a foulness
                        a fullness
            which is splendid
      Marquette
                        was going nowhere
            only the river
      which gathered in the Pekitanoui
            the way Mary received
                  the Holy Ghost
      and he called it
            *La Rivière de la Conception*
where
      on the cliff
                        opposite the jointure
      he saw an image
            "as large as two calves
                                    they have
                        horns
                        on their heads
            like those of a deer
                  red eyes
                        a man's body
            covered with scales
                        and a long tail
      winds all round the
                              body

                    passing above the head
                        and going back
                    between the legs
                            ending in a fish's tail"
                it was red black and green
            as the good Father tells it
                    high above the river


                        on the Illinois side

5

as if the ragged city
        were a passage in strings
consonant
                with a poetry
                                you master
though it tears at the eyes
        when cells
                sing
        the autobiography
        of stone

and a counterwill
                        light
                                soundless
rises as a foretelling of old age
        when cells radiate
                the colors
                        of their music

        dismantling the city
also beautiful
                dismantling
        the importuning will
given to believe
                earth is without edges

        all combat
                        happens
                beyond the edges of the mind
it is in that
                like music
                        and water

"without contradiction
                there would be no world
each form is determined
                by its own particular
                contradiction"

        the earth
        has bubbles
        as water has

and now is the time
         to enter the bubble

    that was the order
(whose order?)
              that love be entangled
         in itself
              so it hath neither
              beginning
                        nor end
    "these dull notes we sing
         discords need
                   for helps
                   to grace them"
    in the antient bokes of ayres
    Campion sings
              this grace to earth it

the edges of music fray
         (the edges of love)
    and that is a kind of mercy
         because in the mind
              the chord
                        unresolved
              is unbearable

    the pace is slow
         and the music
                        generous
    takes time to develop themes
         that seem inconsequential
it is a paradise of loose-ends
    and the music issues
         from a land
    disfigured by the beautiful
corrupted
         by renewal

              but what is done
is a vision that melts
         and leaves the eyes stinging
you have entered a garden
         where you are known

you are its image
                in all that you do
        and common
but you know nothing
                    of its steep
        terraces
                and maze-like
        walks
                go out
        into their own nightmares

        nine young women sit
in an attitude you thought allegorical
        (and you feared them
                        as muses
                who might find you
                    in the flesh
                        wanting)

        but you know them all
            and they speak simply
touching your anger
                as they might
                        brush back
                their hair
        though they sit
                by a fountain
        they knit commonplace
                        socks
and you are drawn to their needles
                which they ply
            thoughtlessly
                as their words
                        turn
        as they count their stitches
        and twist out of themselves

        a hound at the foot of one
            raises its head
                        and whimpers
an old dog
            and smooth-mouthed
    you have lost your habits
            as the dog has

and you are unused
                              to the richness
            of the evening air
            as you watch the light
                              play in the hair
                  of the daughters of Aesop
sitting nightlong
      by the waters
                        the city the stars seem to be
                              reflect the ordinary
                                    mystery
                        most restlessly

      and again she comes to you
            in the shape of a lion
and again
            as a canary
                  in a cage

thickening impatient hands
            of wheezing accordion sky
                  between massed blacks
the cannibal circulation begins
                  earth is water
                        sky is water

      she comes to you
            in the shape of
                  a woebegone hag
in the shape of a child

      feisty incarnations flower
and like flowers
      the music cannot revive them

            you feel
                        behind your eyes
            the first vital stirring
            of death
      as if it were some goddess
            you'll give birth to
                  *olulu*
                  *olulu*

some reckless innocence
     whose perfection
          is tautological
meditates
               in this garden
you have cleared
     with no tool
but your imperfect
                    desire

**6**

the snows come at last
    and the anniversary
        of the old oppressiveness
freighted with two millennia
    of denial of flesh

we have had it backwards
        as a people
it is not the *moral* of the story
    but the endless narrative play
    of the moral
you planned in April to canoe
    the upper Hudson
and studied maps of the river
    thought of strategy
        for the hardest passages
the canoe
    in a white rip—
though the plans for the trip fell through
and were until now forgotten—
    appeared as the vessel
    of a moral
which could not otherwise be known

if what you say
carries any weight
    with the past
it is
    as a canoe
        loaded with wisdom
the encyclopedia
    compiled by careful men
        recommends
    reckless assertion
to piece out a river
    caught in its own bashful
    failure
    to run

and its morality
    is beyond question

as your memory is not
    because you do not know
        if you proposed a canoe trip
    or if the story came to serve a moral
—assume for the time
      you were involved in those plans
    even than the trip was taken—

    now you know
what it is to wait
    not to wait
        for speech
  but to wait in
      the midst
        of speech
which betrays its intention at every turn

  the belly
    of St Louis Woman
begins to grow now
       and her navel protrudes
as if in giving birth
   she must reach out to her own
        sources
and let the child take shape
   in the womb of the history
    which you purvey

  she becomes
     for the time
  Woman
you would not think
  she came from St Louis
as she settles astride
  the immemorial ritual
you wish you were not confronted
  with this child's birth
   at Christmas
it confuses the issue of birth
     and prevents you
  from reaching deftly
  into the crashing heart
    of your own incarnation

       \*    \*    \*

you are engaged
            in benign combat
with a factual being
as if you were both practicing
                        one of the martial arts
            to express an impossible
                            earthliness
                in a stylized
                        violence
            which leaves itself spinning
            in mid-air
                    clockwise
        and counter-clockwise
                    between father
                    and child

        it *means* nothing to you
                it is common
the strut and strength of love
                    is beyond meaning
            this woman means nothing
        the vestments
                        of all you do
            and say
                        are common
        you
                and the falling snow
                are common
        common are the one and the two
common
                are the three
                            without meaning
            you invest nothing
                that is all
                        you want
                for now
        for the common
                        to repeat
                itself
                        and knot
            the common endlessness

to the common
   going out
      into the whim
     of time

# III. MEDITATION

1     Space is—such is its character, its only character, until something moves.

1.2   What basks (O.N. *bathask*, middle voice of *batha*, to bathe) in itself is what brings another space into being, and that is called language.

1.21  Movement directs itself with space (passive voice) or against space (active voice). It is speaking that calls space into motion.

1.3   Language is, as opposed to the monotony of space, tied back to itself and, so, is always in motion.

1.31  It is like counting because each movement is determined by that which it immediately follows and the sequence of which the words are representative.

1.4   The satisfaction of appetite is an event in both space and language, but it does not happen in precisely the same way both here and there.

1.41  The surest nouns are gestures.

1.42  The surest verbs are mimetic.

1.5   Language has exploited the empty spaces between gesture, mimesis, and speech by letting one sign play with or against another.

1.51  That is, language is meaningful because it is caught-up with (such imprecision is unavoidable) the ways by which people get from one place to another. The condition of a language in a given culture-time might be gauged by the ability of the people to give directions to some specific place.

1.6   Language is spacious.

1.7   Space is spacious (this is not a tautology).

1.8   Either space or language can be measured by desire or the contrary of desire. That is, we must assume that the first speech was not spoken. It *happened* where one condition held audience with another.

1.81  To measure either space or language by the contrary of desire is demonic.

1.82  The argument leads to this conclusion: the first mouth was not embodied. It was a nothing which shook, like a peach tree in wind, or stood, like a bear. If that were not the case, we would despair of speaking altogether and sit under a peach tree, eating peaches as they fell.

1.82 A peach pit would be the first act of language, but not language itself.

1.83 A love letter composed of peach pits would be a statement of intense devotion.

1.9 To imagine is an infinite act of language which extends into and completes itself in space.

1.91 To be of genius is an infinite act of space which thrusts out into and expends itself in language.

2 Language is limited, as space is not. Where-you-are is limited, as what you say is not. The proposition, "I have counted six bears," cannot be verified by the person who has seen only five, but it can believed.

2.1 What-you-say has been confused with language; where-you-are has been confused with space. These mistakes have been the cause of much suffering.

2.2 The first words were "earth" and "sky'": signs which diverged in meaning from one another. Stories of the Genesis have to do with the history of language. The Earth has always been without meaning and always will be. That is not a mystery, it is a fact.

2.21 It follows that the aboriginal syntax related all things to a moving axis perpendicular to the earth.

2.22 The axis was called SMOKE because it rose and RAIN because it fell.

2.23 SMOKE and RAIN were forms of language. Their approximate meanings were the hand which opens downward (SMOKE) and the hand which opens upward (RAIN).

2.24 One could speak of "the hands of language" and be roughly in keeping with the ancient usage.

2.25 The conjugations are "the first finger of RAIN, the second finger of RAIN. . . , the thumb of RAIN, as well as, the first finger of SMOKE," etc.

2.26 The syntactical forms would include forearm, shoulder, the headbone connected to the neckbone.

2.27 To speak is not to have but to *be* a body. The proper study of language is physiology.

2.3 The ploy of culture was to moralize the primal differentiations (that Uranos was castrated by a son playing out a neurotic fantasy).

2.4 The rites which were instituted to enact that morality are in their intent contrary to the requirements of the syntactical form known as the joining of hands (another act of separation and distinction, although the terminology is misleading to us, so completely we have lost *touch* with these origins).

2.5 You or I arrive in the space between hands reaching for one another.

2.6 The present era should be properly known as The Passage of Short Arms.

2.7 In this time we have a life which is more frankly thought-about than lived. It may be sung. It cannot be known.

# IV. THE BULL

1

I was talking of nothing
yet found no way
to say
      take this hand
of SMOKE and this
         of RAIN

      fingers stretched
an inch of blue flame
between our thumbs

the brute indifference
an inch
      a distance

I speak
of an inclination
pitching
      down
roof-like
        to an icy cavern
a cake
a chair
     to sit in
head cocked
    to the left
    eyeing a crack
in the wall
       of grammar

consider
     the shape of a deer
in ochre
with heavy balls
and long teeth

the least of my worries
were the screens
to cut
     and say

this one
     say
  that

take a knife
in hand
    to write
your pleasure
   say
as of then
now
   now
you wait
     again
unfold

   November
cannot come again
to your cone of
   yellow light
lay out
   say

and malarial
      swamps
   Spanish moss
the cypress
the cry of fingers
in touch to know

   now seized
by the eye of malady
the feet of clay

2

I am a hive
        of myself
moving as bees
in my words
        and jeans

        the children
will be
more patient
than we
who go
through the fields
where the oil
wells grow
to wonder
if some
frontier
force

still

3

thinking again
    it is over
and it seems to be
for a time
    we say
that's over

    but it is
another way
            to say
it is so far:
    I'd not know
whether to go
        east
    or west
to get there

living in Kansas
    it was west
and we said
    Ho Chi Minh
is marching
    down the Turnpike

he has raped
    and looted
in Topeka
    he has
embraced
    Ceres
of the State House
he was only
thirty-five miles
    west
and we would
    welcome him
and love him
    as our child

\*      \*      \*

once we went
        to meet him
and in our dis-
        appointment
he was not there
        we marched
to the Capital
        chanting
what else?
        He was not
there
        but his name
rang in the streets

he was
        further west but
that was the edge
        of our imagi-
                nations
and if he were
        elsewhere
he was
        no use to us

        but now
May Day
and the spring rains
have come to New York

        we cannot go
                to Ho City
any more than we can dance
        the May Pole
properly dressed

        this is not
the end

it's the beginning
        we wait for
and adore
                our waiting
        our butts

drag in the dust
     because
our left hand
     doesn't know
what our right hand
is doing

4

A Dream of Ho Chi Minh

I had read his book
        and when I met him
I was surprised
            he was simian

—I kept trying
to let a question
form there
            in the air
between us
            to say
how did you get
that much beauty
behind those eyes
        but in place
of asking
I took
his hand

    his fingers
were long
    and hairy

he said
something polite
        he said
you must want
    to wash up
after your journey

you have come
    so far

5

from the top
        of Nebo
he saw
            grapes
growing

        so I am now
thinking
            waiting
for the news

            May 1, 1975
                5:43 p.m.

        I can't afford
sentimentality
                    now

        the saints
are playing
                catch
in the alley-way

the baseball
                broken
at the seam
        begins
        to unravel
so when it is thrown
it whirs
        like a covey
                of quail
in flight

6

    as the Marines
evacuated
        the last Americans
from Ho City
    Graham Martin burned
47 thousand crisp green
      one-hundred dollar bills

    was that the ritual
completion
    of the Revolution?

or was it here
        today
when the forsythia
   came into bloom?

the evening news

nerve
      6:30 p.m.

   out the bathroom
      window
along Pine Street
   three trees
hanging
     with large
   red balls

   the Ambassador
was eating an apple
     as he spoke
   he hadn't expected
and so forth

   he saw it
as a swarm of locust
   he was that far away
from earth

7

the cop's boots
    were buckled
        to his knees
and the brass studs
    gathered
            the falling sun

his helmet
            was
vizored
        he wore
an ammunition belt
    across his chest

but the authority
        of the sun
did not extend
        to his eyes
they did not shine

    and when it began
        to rain
he shook his head
            and drank
    a cup of acid
        he drained
from the battery
    of his bike

    some said he
smiled
        some said
he did not
            smile

I
  did not see him
smile
        that is the first
stage
    of knowledge

the mayor
saw him smile
and he is Dutch

8

Saturday
        they will crown
The Tulip Queen
            I think
someone will walk
        around Washington Park
wearing wooden shoes

        I realize now
that the closest way
to Ho Chi Minh City
        might be
                    north

    9:18 p.m.

they make sandals
        by drawing their feet
on discarded tires
        and cut out soles
which they strap
                to their toes

shoeing themselves
        as we cover
                        our hands
        both right
                    and left
        SMOKE
                and
RAIN

The Great
            Circles
        O-
void
        of Earth
                egg
        I could hold
            two of them
one
    in each hand

9

coming
  and going
they wait
  for the
Red Cross

  Smoke
    and
      Rain

F IRE

  in Ho City
the army patrols
  the streets
    unarmed

compare
  as act
the way Bob Gibson
    pitched
  in the 1967
    World Series

  his fast ball
so alive
  no other act
could surpass it

  we watched
      in the autumn
sun
  open-mouthed
not saying anything
    our mouths
  hanging open
to show
  how some speech
    was required
like actors
  who had dropped
    their lines

we became an audience
    to ourselves

    compare the bowl
of Busch Stadium

    and the streets
so occupied
       where they run
through Ho City
        and out
into the rice fields

    —May 2, 1975
     11:09 A.M.

10

Adam's mouth was a map
he was the schwa in his own mouth
and the full-voiced vowels
Lords of the Cardinal Directions

but let us skip over
the deformation and decay

blood runs through our sentences
from noun to noun
the verbs are covered in gore

—May 3, 1975

# V. STEAM

V. STEAM

VARIATIONS

red
door
painted black

washed
in orient
and hung out

to dry
eyes
like oil

the sun
stung
and blued them

blind
masque of me
gentle knight

of the dark
hearse
and black flowers

\*

red door
forced
after head

occludes
the moon
mad

for the tedious
black
eclipse

the hole
in earth
opens

the whole moon
begins
to glow

from center
out
and you reenter

saying
that world
absorbs

all color
bathe yourself
sable-coupled

in the soak
of hostile
desire

*

bottle
of whiskey
blunt

knife
a surgical
door

the doctors
of darkness
broken

and the wait
for recovery
doubting

what's beyond
the door
knowing

the door's
a hand
wanting to

shake it
we are
nostalgic

for our own
hopeless
time

*

I
have not
seen

the angel
who stands
at the black

door
after the redness
drains

I have not
seen
an angel

but I believe
she would
look like

Lillian Gish
tied
to a railroad

track
the ropes
would be

white wings
and the cross-
ties rungs

on a ladder to
heaven
where the interior

teases
and song
is an ugly

car
driven recklessly
perfected

despair
is a high
way

to the center
of earth
black

and red
my coat is
my time

And when I was twelve my grandfather took me back to Granby, Missouri, where he was raised. The mining company was using the small school, where he had his only education, as a tool shed, and his anger flared out against the owners, brilliant and hard, after forty years.

He had walked, he told me, by his father, from the school, up the creek, to the spring, where the horses were tied, walked closely, to keep the sheriff, who was standing about where we were, from shooting.

I did not think to ask what the agony was, but now I let it all close in: the whole of the past, the law, the romance of ancestors who worked beneath the ground.

3

I dreamt of sleeping
with you beside me
both of us sleeping quietly
as we were
precisely as we were
Lois' drawing
*After Ingres*
the fat nude
was askew
on the bone-white wall
the bottom to the left
as it was
the dirty socks
dropped together
near the foot of the bed
did not appear to be hands
folded in prayer

the mantle clock
began to strike
the name
of the eighteenth century
craftsman who made it
is not known
but he signed himself
with a device
which may be a hand
pierced by three knives

a radical authority
inhabits our house
as it is
we have this time

**4**

remembered
             again
I don't look with your eyes

        out
             the bathroom window

houses cluster
                 slight misproportions
leave me gasping
        for a place my eyes can rest

the architecture
                     does not constitute
a street
          south
                 along Pine Street

I'm not talking aesthetics
        it's a practical fact

             the wet pavement
        and up to the begrimed clouds

                 that's no grounds
                 for an argument

5

after eight years this lust
leaves us both sometimes
bleeding still

the teeth of loving you
the teeth of loving—
the poem walks on two feet

sometimes we do
the poem comes to replace us
it says
      for the time

you are not required
              or
you are required elsewhere
it burns for us
        it is us

the ear curled
remorsely in the head
does hear

I do speak
      if I am impure
the poem also speaks falsely
lost
    I come back to you

they say
      he did not find himself
he was a tooth
        a broken tooth
but lying beside you last night

unable to sleep
I could not tell if it were you
or I
   who was breathing

# VI. THE LAST DAYS

1

moon full
out over the Hudson
I am restless
sleepless
walk up
and down
the stairs

waiting in nerves
the moon
the soprano voice sings
a language I do not understand

a gale
dry snow
blowing on the street
sky scaled above the moon
with cold white clouds

I am restless in wind
windows
rattle
house is warm
2 a.m.

the kitchen is inhabited
dirty dishes
are real

what else?
I pour a cup of coffee
climb the stairs
breathe

what would I give up for total concentration?

a
serious wind
house shudders
nerves
of the house
end in frozen ground

nerves end
      breathe

   the dark is full of sounds
I can only say
        I am no longer addressed
I am poised at the inner-edge of names
the nerve of things
        I recite the poem
St Louis Woman
       grits her teeth
           she
    has the poem by heart
    has me
      by heart
she knows what happens
I found a blank
     in imagination
and filled it
     with the two of us
(one last swallow of
      coffee
        in the cup)

   this is the apocalypse
the moon is full
      climbing to mid-heaven
and claims the sky
   behind the scale of clouds

   down the stairs
the weary chords of the storm windows
   tuned to my
       restlessness
   one more time
    pour the coffee
breathe
   up the stairs

  I say
the hypnotic miles of
     the night-long headlights

flickering in our westward eyes
    are beads
        on a rosary
    we must someday tell

Interstate 70
        from Columbus westward
runs with miserly
        economy
    Springfield Indianapolis Effingham
are places
        only in their listless assertion
that the answer to Heidegger's question
        "Why is there something
            rather than nothing?"
    is after all simple

    if we plunder them
        for a bed
            or a meal
that does not reveal an obedience
        I must be clear
the accidents have been demons
    in a divine but
        remote
            mind

if the roads
    lead
    into towns
        that are tenuous
            and ugly
in their collusion with time
    they dry
        the wet wings
    of a memory
        so perfect
    in its uselessness
that it stutters
        the obvious
        names
I want a clear mind
    so cluttered
    with landscape

I am the landscape and
        the metabolism of travel
      is a clock in the rear-view mirror
      I want a clear mind
because those who live near death
        are gentle
and have a shamble-footed grace
    superior
       in some of its moves
   to the ritual dances
     the lurid danger
   the chance
      by which I am here

## 2

the old habits are not lost
they occur now
                as climbing roses
            on a chain-link fence
between a state of mind
        and what I have to do

    I learned to count
and numbering
                devil-may-care
        disciplines
                    leads back
across a territory
                which the circuit
                    of love
                lifted
                        from melody
        so I know the words must rise

    the chorus—I will call it
        "the land itself"
                knowing no other name—
is the glory I hear
                    in
                    or behind
        the flock of northbound geese

    I do not know
            who is speaking
but it is I

        St Louis Woman comes
        brooding
                on a wronged world
    measuring the losses
                    by her rightness

    my eyes are shaded
            by a hand that is not mine
but one that reaches out
                through sockets of birthdays

                *       *       *

she holds the carved thigh-bone
                    of habit
                in her hand
the pity
          of a forgotten story
the hand
              she says
                    carved its time
along its enemy's leg
          these are the parts of a clock
the archeology of body
                recovers shards
                    of a continent mastered
count by this
          it is
                and was
                    your history

I would write what happens
                                I say
on my own thigh-bone
          to walk balanced
                            upon its tactlessness

but this bone
                  shows the way
along a stream
                to a place
where an ancient cottonwood cleaves the sky
          it *must* be cottonwood
                  otherwise it could not stand
                  so mutely
because the sky
                above
                        is heavy
as the heart might be
          on a less propitious day

I lead you
                back
                        through a course of events
not adding up
          but marking them

with my hand
                    the gestures blaze a trail
whatever hunger I feel
        on behalf of a savage lateness
                issues here
        at the literal joints
                the particles of speech
bending phonemes together

        this neat thigh-bone
                            pictures
            a troubled kinship
the readiness of heart tells
                        tolls
                the coming land tide
I do not know I am ready
        but these gestures reveal a ripe
                        dangerous pulse
the lame march of events
                        measures me
we are almost out
                of the timber
the spirit of harshness
                the eyes opening
        in rush of time

        count them
can you number
                these eyes
        in the bramble?

3

I do not remember what I meant
when I carved the Pech de L'Aze bone
230,000 years ago
it was just a bone
it came from a fine ox
I recall the ox
fat
red
its hind-quarters
were puddles of flesh spread
when it lay on the ground

it was an inclement day
in spring
late March or
early April
as if it weren't enough
to say something
to the bone
I wrote on it

I don't remember what I said
the encyclopedia doesn't say
and St Louis Woman says
it wasn't important
whatever it was

we slaughtered the ox
when she was heavy with child
its flesh was red
the color of crushed berries
and the flames were
another
red
orange and red
when the fat dropped
on the logs
it flared up
white and blue
the tip of the flame
reaching up
toward the meat

                        was green

            it was warmer then
weather is the edge
                        of the outside
            it is not metaphor
            it was a rattle of voice
            I recorded
            all the care is inside
                        the rattle


            it was no
                        necessary truth
I carved on the bone
            the name
                        of the ox perhaps
            a census
                        a consensus
                                    a tally
the care
            taken inside the city
            to trace the lines
                        like the streets
                        on the bone
            it was no accident
I was bored
            and amused myself
                        with purpose


it was before
                        I heard the voice
                                    speaking
the dead question of the bone
            like the City on the High Plains:
                        the riddle does not exist
it is a dead bone
                        become by chance
                                    a question
            even as it is asked
            by a wise voice
                        the dreams misled me
the wise man
            stood barefoot
                        in the snow

4

the City is no joke
it is the rods
and cones
of my eyes
sitting on the 100th meridian
flicking out dangerously
like a silky
heavyweight's left
or time

and the mountains
behind it
are the breath of confusion
so a morality play
takes place
between them
on the high arid
stage of western Kansas

confusion is cast
in the role
of a temptress
and now
that it is I
who is speaking
she moves in
and her perfumes
are the smells
black earth
heavy voluptuous soil
ripe to the plough
she is the embodied presence
of sham fertility
and wears a smile
as a chemise
which covers neither
her lust
nor the splendour
of her parts

*   *   *

Innocence is unclothed
before her
                    and their mutual ecstasy
           is another character
                              he recites
the entries of the encyclopedia
           loving each of them
                              he
           cannot take them
           in any order
                              than B
                    follows A
                       as C
                    follows B


           he thinks to find his name there
realized
                    amidst the names of presidents
                              and flowers
the resolute tellings
                    of times
                    and places
                              marked
                    but not
                              marked-off


           her beauty
                    is undeniable
and his
           fragile
           is willing to thrive
                              in chaos


           in the lyric
                    of the great brown volumes
a world ranges round
                              screaming orders
           six more deadly sins
                    each wearing a handsome coat
dance
           the Nutcrackers Rag
                              and I see them
spelling out my name

in the lurid figures
                of their dance
the close
            oppressive sky
        reflects their dancing
the arthritic
                confusion of bone
as I hobble
            to my test

        for a time
the audience
                loses confidence
            in the outcome
it seems that Innocence
        is not simply
                    excluded
        it truly has no place
as the alphabetic
                    configurations
            are trucked off
                        to hell
the grim smiles
                ache
                    on their faces


        and when he turns his eyes
out
        to a vacant lot
                    a cathedral rises
walled with clarity of mind
        and domed with corruption

        "This"
                he says
                        "I will call 'Paradise'
I will be utterly commodious with myself
    I will marry St Louis Woman
            because we are the survivors
        perhaps the only ones
            and we will live
                    in this church

until the destruction of the earth
ends"

the audience
shrinks back
until it is so far away
and airy
it may be only a cloud
between here
and the mountains
the old habits
lay
on the theater floor
like dropped programs
and silk handkerchiefs
and the whole of my homeland
is an accusation

5

I do the dance
                of waiting now
the words are prepared
        they are a crib
                in which the child will sleep
unencumbered moves
        of both feet
                        find
                                difference
                in indifference
                                the beginning
                of rhythms
        to make the City ring
                with bells that do not exist

I have memorized half
                of the encyclopedia
and can render it
                        in dactylic hexameters
        without belief

        with nothing
                        but this woman
and a child not yet born—
                it was a lovely wedding
        St Louis Woman
                blushing behind her veil
        and six-months pregnant—
the child comes
                from a place so near
        it's always almost here
being
        and not-being swaddled together
                its butt in one hand
                its head in the other

        the encyclopedia
                        will not sell
one prospect said
                "We know too much

we
      are crowded in
                     by facts
            out by facts
                     I don't care
            I don't care
            Nothing is told in your books
                     that I want to know"


      and I did not care
or I cared for nothing
                     but the smells
            of the street
      the thunderstorm
                  moving in
            over the mountain
      and the possibility of walking out
                  on her crowded dilemma
      and back
                  to the waiting
nothing else makes sense now
      but to do the dance
            which is a release from thinking
I have found a New Place
      and I call it "I Am"
            it is a City on the High Plains


      I sit beside St Louis Woman
who laughs
            at my concern
                  and unbuttoned mind
her eyes are instructions
            in a kind of ecstasy
      which has nothing to do with the child
who has a life
            and random selection
                  of genes


      dreams come to me
                        and spread
the feast of love
                  on the ground
      the love juice

drips down
my chin

"There is no archetypal melody"
and no archetypal
dance
the dance now
does not wait
for the child
it is clean
and pure
as I wait
I feast here

6

the moon
misguides
        the heart
in risible
    untimely
        ways

and when it is full
I do not sleep
    I am not sure
                tonight
which of these women
    draws me
        through the lucid
hands
    and fingers
        of myself

    St Louis Woman sits
holding Anne
            who holds communion
    with Earth
she changes nothing
    she is her own immaculate
absorption
            in alimental concerns
    her birth
birth itself
        is the most common fact
it leaves nothing to say
    or everything we say
        is about it
a metaphor
            to the harsh
                objective spring
    of meat
            into light
blinking
        at the cold radiance
of the eye

            *    *    *

it was not my birth
as I thought it might be
empty
dumb
before the fact of her
I thought only
that she should be wrapped
and held
I see now
that speech
not breath
is the soul of confusion
we are damned
to talk
non-sense
for the most part
faced with the brute silence
and failure of molecular bonds

we pass
through a City of Words
syntactical nerves
wordy eyes
we make a mystery of birth
St Louis Woman says
so death can be a mystery

the silence
rises
from inside
and claims
the grammar
first the object
then the subject
in the final deathless verb

only the moon
and I
are awake now
Anne occasionally purrs
in her sleep

\*     \*     \*

              let me say
I intend to cheat death
        to get the silence
                        there
              between the words

        if as an old man
        I sit quietly
                    in the sun
I will have talked
                    my way
        out of the City
        and there
                    my love
        will be uncontaminated
                        by myself
        I will sit by a wall
            cracking words
                            like peanuts
                between my thumb
                and forefinger
until the silence
        becomes as common as hulls
dropped at my feet

        but in the meantime
we need
            new stories
to tell the children